Dedicated to my Grandfather Late Sh. Dina Nath Gandhi

A prolific Urdu writer.

Introduction

How much do we know about Love? Can we measure the innocent smile of a red rose that is the same for everyone? Or the fragrance of it that is similar in spring and winters. Is that what is Love? Indeed, a yes. Whatever- it is spectacular.

Change is getting so much real and everywhere to be seen yet the least appreciated. We don't treasure it, as we want to live a life of comfort with adequate freedom. Today, do we even get the time to enjoy that comfort and independence? Have you ever stopped at the sight of a red rose and if yes; how many times did you look at it smiling at you? You can just count will be just enough like the fingers in your hands. I ask again, therefore, "How much you know about love"? We don't even change for our good and thus we remain unmoved to even feel the emotion of Love. Change outside, inside, and far and wide that has always existed will remain forever as the fundamental law of nature is never a part of our nature, so we need to do what we love and change ourselves to be able to do what we love and live for, is a measure of what we need to achieve

This short story is on change and the idea is to make people help themselves to accept, appreciate and embrace change outside and inside and in the process of it, enjoy life to its absolute potential. It tells us how crucial it is in our lives and merely enduring it means resisting life.

There are short stories in each chapter with a message and how you can change what you need to change followed by concrete steps on how to achieve it. **I, as a protagonist,** tell the story and I am known to the principal character of the story. Later, I leave a message at the end of each chapter and allow my readers to contemplate upon it as if it was their story. Finally, I tell them what they need to learn and how to employ those steps to bring an impact to their lives. In just knowing what they are missing is good enough for them to change.

The aim has been to make readers assist themselves so that they start loving life, a life of struggle, a life of challenges that will get sorted the day they bring in the action through a change in their life. Those who will identify this will remain always magnanimous in their thoughts and actions, exalted in their love for life that will never cease to exist.

Another key aspect of this book is that each chapter has a story that is connected to the title of the chapter and I have attempted to put across a message as a moral of the story for my readers. Further, each chapter in some amount shows the general disliking for change- like a love gone wrong; to the ultimate bliss of finding yourself.

The journey is all about one’s insecurities and fears towards change. Change never comes effortless and has a price of discomfort to pay, a sacrifice like any return on investment that will not be immediate, and with many reasons for one to remain in one's comfort zone. It has sufficient reasons for you to appreciate change, embrace it, and ways to measure one’s success as never done before to finally feeling like a winner is established.

Chapter 1

Understanding Change

There was a man called Mahesh. He was of a strong built and worked as an Engineer in a reputed firm. He was a happy man because he felt he had two sons and earned just good enough to take care of his family. His wife Rohini was a clerk in the administrative department of a small office in Delhi.

Mahesh was a contended person and didn't complain much. His wife was always by his side. She was ideal at least for any husband expecting a working wife who was obedient and a dedicated Hindu wife. Mahesh always took pleasure in how he took care of his family, and with particular reference, he never missed to tell in public how respectful his two sons were. His larger-than-life praise of his wife often was interrupted with a look upon of disbelief and envy by many around. At times some would take benefit of the situation and order a delicacy in the name of his wife that he would not object upon. He was heard often flattering her wife and saying that she listens to her and never argues with him was now and then waited to be heard by some who would then leave not before they treat their taste buds. In recent times, this is sufficient reason for one to be a happy man. They don't make wives like that anymore.

However, his happiness was not without an end. His elder son though dedicated left for the USA and after doing his masters in biotechnology had different aspirations and settled there. Another secret desire that surfaced afterward was when he refused to return to India and gave an explanation to his father for his wanting him to return to India for a cup of tea; the tea of love and togetherness. His attention to his arrogance and his fondness for being around with his friends and always flattering his wife did cost him extremely. His son never returned. The younger son too after his marriage left for Bangalore to an IT firm.

Mahesh lives now with his old wife who has mellowed down with age and she is exceedingly thankful to live that change in her. She has no qualms in life for at least she has known Mahesh better now. He on the other hand has remained the same and didn't grow up with age, rather keeps shouting for trivial things. Moreover, he has become neglectful with old age. There are verbal quarrels in the air that are heard wherein many times he is kept mouth shut by a snap from Rohini that you are sick. My friends, it's difficult to defeat ladies in a squabble and very difficult and almost out of the question when she is your wife. This sickness needs no medicine as her sharp tongue was enough an answer for him. Now he sulks though it's too late, thinking that this change in her wife is not doing any good to him. She has changed herself now and this transform in her has liberated her in many ways. Mahesh has lost a lot who has failed to change and lives in a make-belief world of his own. His confidence is getting lesser with each passing day and the tables have turned now with Rohini who is heard many times dominating him and disagreeable about his ways that she hates him more than ever before.

Moral of the story

Change is life, everything grows. Your children also grow to an adult just like you or maybe if not like you. Your opinion of yourself, your conceit also need a change with times; better we become unassuming and start accepting change around us, and then only we can make people feel that change around them. The change is what we give them so that they feel easy, independent, and love the life around them.

Understanding Change- One never likes to change. We don't even accept changes in our lives- big or small. The last thing we want to do to ourselves is not to accept change. We are taught that change is ever happening and we even feel its presence around. We see buds grow into blossoming flowers and in the same way, we see our children grow and enjoy the change in them from a teenager to an adult, and then with strings attached of our aspirations for them to become a Doctor, Engineer, or an IAS officer or even an MBA; the list goes on. Chiefly, above all the rest, we wish a dedicated child out of them. There is no fault to think that way as a parent, conversely, are we ensuring that we bring them up as independent individuals who are capable enough to take care of them by themselves. We dream about things that will change no matter, and when we see nothing changes is when we are puzzled and we start thinking as if something wrong has happened and we were ordained to get this.

By that time it is late to change or maybe too late. The fact of the matter is that we did grow up and not on intellect. We didn't change our attitude to feel the way others do and many times dominated them to the level that we could not draw a line when the sense of self did set in and we became a story of just me, me, and me. The love for liberty and peace is always what we as humans thrive for and when we achieve it, we cross all boundaries of love and togetherness. Change is not what you want to change in others but what you can change within to make others around you feel your presence as always welcoming.

Steps to Understand Change

1. Feel the changes around you and love them.
2. Listen to others well to understand how different they are from you.
3. Your aspirations are yours, never mix with others.
4. Dreams become a reality and not understanding what is change and how it can bring your dreams closer to reality is just like daydreaming that is far from reality. This way even the dreams never surface.
5. Live your dreams by living in reality, changing yourself maybe if implausible but understanding change is good enough for you to start- at least living your dreams is very important.

Chapter 2

It is all about you and me

Sonia was an educated young woman in her mid-thirties. She was a lawyer by profession and a social activist for child exploitation who was waging a long ending war against it. It is today guarded to a large extent from what it was a decade back in 2011 but is still rising. Sonia at that time was even busier in her profession and was at no difficulty in her work, and with her clients who were all in applauds of hers. She of late started becoming argumentative than ever before and it went even outside the walls of the courtroom to her home. She was very much into the noble service of working for children that she used to come late- detrimental she felt many times being a woman; she could not help herself.

Her husband Karan was a recognized businessman who loved his family more than anything else; even more than his business sometimes. It was an inherited legacy to him as if money was just a means to an end and not everything. One day he filed for a divorce with Sonia. They had a daughter Rashmi, who now was 10 years old. Sonia herself a notable lawyer could not change her fate. She lost the love of her life- her child and her husband after she lost her protection and the case to him in 2017 and then everything changed from thereupon in her life. She cried many times but in vain. Still, she continued her fight persistently and with a deep conviction as her purpose of life, had become deep-seated in her. Her love for her child though remained but was never enough to facade deep in the heart of Rashmi when she needed her most.

Sonia met me one summer day in June. I run an NGO for kids who are abused and in one of such cases on child rights was for one child Vishal, as his protection was yet not decided from his separated parents who had deserted their love of life for an extra-marital. Mother was a housewife and their father disowned Vishal and now the child's decision was left to his parents or at the best left for an NGO. I saw her after two decades. She was not that very striking anymore as times did change a lot for her. The smile of hers still didn't age and was full of love, care, and acceptance that smiled on me and I was taken aback by the thought of it. She was elated that day and was speeding up back to get home a little early because Rashmi, her only daughter called her after 15 years and it was her marriage the next day. I had no words for my high regard for her and her joy for her daughter to meet her as if she had found her true love. It looked to me for all those few years I had known her as if time had stopped for a while to salute her that day. I could not hold my tears in admiration for that moment of joy in which her love for her family was building up that never could surface well.

She exclaimed –"How are you, Sir". Good to see you after that long. A grin she had and then she said again, "Please if you may excuse me for a day or two as I have to rush for my daughter's wedding celebration the next day. You have known all and I can't wait anymore and just say goodbye to you today. Please don't mind, we can meet again on the day after tomorrow". It was her day of re-union. I was exceptionally happy however my eyes were wet and before I could say anything she had left. I felt that some stories never change and such stories of love and reunion never go wrong. It was like a measure of how much she achieved that was way ahead of any figures. She was not beaten by the ugly turns of life. She changed those times. She is a story for you and me.

Moral of the story

Life is never easy. It is the fruits of our good and bad karma. Karma means our actions. What we think, we become and that is how we act all the time. Some believe it is the effects of our past life so we endure in this life however a lot of saints say we can change this life with our good manners and so even our destiny. Sonia's life depicts a life of love for others, selfless service, and a change she embraced and cherished all her life. She was knocked down by the turns in her life but she was up again and maybe because those changes could not shake her or take her away from her love for life; a life she was living for others, a life that she breathed each day to alter the lives of many children around her; even if that had a huge price to pay. Nonetheless, she is called with all the reverence and love from her daughter so she is a winner all the way, and all well that ends well. This story is all about you and me. It is all about enduring agony but with fortitude. Be prepared for the worst as life is a lesson learned the hard way. Change is sometimes to make you walk the path that is long and needs your full dedication. It may make you a winner or a loser but you will be always remembered for the hope that you ignited in the lives of many others. The life you get is the life you chose and in the end, you are always a winner because you never ran away from the changes that allow you to live a full life. It's not only a bed of roses for you but what bed of roses you can offer to the world. Her tears didn't matter to her much till she kept herself busy improving their lives that wiped their tears.

Steps to know Change is about you and me

1. You are never alone. Your story can be a story that is being shared by many others whom you didn't even meet in this life.

2. Change is real and is not always a bed of roses. You mustn't move away from righteousness as it is the test of God on you. You have to pass this test of your inner-awakening where God resides. Remain true to yourself and you will win.

3. If you are a victim of change, there is a reason for this. Stay deep-rooted, do not lose hope as there is always a bigger story you may unfold that may change your life for yourself and many others.

4. Change itself is a life you never lived before. After understanding change, try to accept and treasure it and even more than that be the change you want to see in others. Change is a destiny re-lived wherein you are the audience as well as the actor. Laugh and celebrate as an audience in all your sufferings as your actions may not be just your act but the act to entertain many others that may tomorrow fill up the cinema halls you never thought of.

5. Your story should be a story of change for many others irrespective of its endings like the Joan of Arc or Madame Currie. The life of change that you accepted may not be a bed full of roses but surely maybe a bed full of roses for generations to come. This was her story. This can be your story too.

Chapter 3

Resist Change to invite miseries

Once upon a time, there was a King called Yashwardhana in the city of Jodhpur. He was a powerful king and I was in his courtyard as an able minister. He always used to listen to me. He was praised for his leadership skills and his ability to act speedily and resist change. His name just like the true meaning of the word was called upon many times, and all across the city people spoke of his popularity. He was undefeated and therefore was feared by many rulers. His administrative skill with my guidance was well appreciated by his friends and envied by his enemies alike.

One day as he sat with me alone in the courtroom and we were discussing laying a wall that strong across the fort of Jodhpur that enemies could not even think to invade it and if by any chance they did, they would by then have little energy left to wage a long war. We started building a wall of hope in the form of a fortress and it was finally completed by the end of the year.

All happened as we had thought. The attempts to seize Jodhpur were now next to impossible and the king started becoming relaxed and started devoting much of his time in his past times and his extra-curricular activities of dining with wine, women, and luxuries that were becoming the talk of the town. He failed to analyze on time that some enemies who had remained quiet for that long were opening an attack from all the fronts and because they had allied with other neighbouring states for a befitting reply to him; was to win and share the plunder later. Once I even tried to tell the king but he had by then made a world of his comforts as a place for all to live and let live and that was very unlikely of a king. On another occasion, he sent me back saying "NOTHING CAN CHANGE THIS CHANGE". Finally, the allied forces attacked him from all fronts, captured him, and later ordered him to have him killed.

Moral of the story

The doom that the king met was not because he wasn't brave enough, or he didn't have leadership qualities, or even not because he was inebriated in his comforts after the fort was built. The reason for his downfall was in his words I realized later when he uttered- "NOTHING CAN CHANGE THIS CHANGE". Your downfall is evident in your endeavours when you stop to think further and do not act upon the changes you made. No change is final and in fact change itself is never final. Your resistance to accepting change firstly is fatal and is full of miseries however, if you are wise enough to change for your benefit that leads to results, it is pointless to become complacent. It is this time for you to act wiser and get the best of support from your friends, well-wishers, or from the ministers to build or cling to your victory stronger and longer. Also as was mentioned that no change is final, your change may not be just yours alone but a reason for a change for many others including your enemies. Isn't this the same today on how businesses are run? You make a product embark on and in a while, many others follow suit and the competition turns in a few years from a monopoly to an oligopoly to a perfect competition by the end. There is such a perfect competition for a change. The change for the market share results in the change of your share, and the final doom when you stop to change further is when your enemies run you down. The competition here and meeting your end is just like king Yashwardhana fall or a story of any firm today from riches to rags.

Steps to know how one may overcome resistance to change and be happy.

1. The measure of your success is not in making a wall of your arrogance and achievements and then spending your time later in your achievements of the past. It is in knowing your present and how well you are placed in it and not getting beaten by yourself in your self-conceit and laurels. Change your present by not resting on your laurels alone but resisting all temptations that take you away from your goals. Change is never final as your success may be an impetus for others to start a journey and for another to invade you. Change itself is all-pervasive and always has a lesson for you. This lesson is to move on and not rest at any place for a very long as that would mean throwing yourself to temptation like the king. It is better to aim at the moon while seeing the sky.

2. Listen to well-wishers and listen to your life-force and realize that grass always looks greener on the other side. Don't stop learning and learn to implement a change of what you learned. If you can learn this, then the change will be far more significant to you and many others.

3. Your success without a yardstick is no success. Your success is what you achieve by the changes you made. However, at the same time when you rested on your laurels, another and even

a higher benchmark is achieved by yet another. The king's enemies in the past or the competition in present times do not allow you to rest. The rest is not the gratification of present times alone; for that, you have all the money and you are not like a king in present times that you would need a fortress to guard your territories. Your role definitely and still is like a king and maybe much beyond it. King and you- the entrepreneur both will have the time to enjoy the luxuries but better if you have them enjoyed for not outside your goals because unlike the king Yashvardhana, your territories have no boundaries and neither are the incessant opportunities for you and many others including your competition and thus leaving you with a bigger role to carry out. The stage set today and presently has a much bigger role than your thoughts could take you and still smaller than the threats that may unfold on you.

4. Resistance to anything including change means accepting a smaller life of you. It is like telling a dead man to walk. It is like resting when nothing is resting and it is like accepting everything relaxing. If anything takes you away from your comfort zone and if that is a change desired but not accepted; it is like a life not accepted. It is no life as the very spirit of life is to feel life growing, changing, and making its way into the world. You don't like your baby to remain a baby even when you know that this change is full

of hardships for him nor would you like to pluck a red-rose that is up-and-coming to its maturity so that you may reap its benefit of fragrance when it blossoms in your heart by the sight of it. How can you resist change without knowing what it has is in store for you in the future? You are merely fearing change and procrastinating that any change is to change your routine. Your liking for such autonomy is a dead mindset that is only opening your doors to misery and is just like accepting defeat without waging a war. Your mind has to widen and open. To get a new job or to start a new business - the changes you would do in your life will change your life by getting you a new job or starting a new venture as your present change for a future unknown. It is far better like a future you envisaged that otherwise would not have been the way you thought it to be if you didn't change it today.

5. Change itself can change the change. This very nature of change makes things attain quality, lean, or even six-sigma. The plan do check and act or the PDCA approach by Deming is thc Deming cycle in theory the world knows but if you go deeper and learn practically, lies the measure of your success. This is a way for you to measure not only what you achieved monetarily in terms of wealth you created for yourself and your family as one, but is the very essence of your existence; alone makes you self-actualize yourself as it

measures not your wealth and your achievements alone. It measures you in your lifetime; your willingness to change and your change for a better you is a stronger you in a living you, who didn't just compromise to exist. Isn't that much happier of you?

Chapter 4

Making success a Habit or a Chance

There was once a young teenager –Rahul who was not from a very well-to-do family. His father was a drunkard and he could hardly pay for a decent living for his family. Rahul was good in sports and wanted to be a wrestler but his father had a different view or no dreams for him. Poverty is a crime. Rahul's elder brother who was Gaurav was favoured all the time as his father always rested on Gaurav's achievements and was unfair towards Rahul. I was working as a coach in a wrestling academy who was building body-builders. One day, Rahul came to me on his bicycle as a broken and crying teenager of 14 years who was fed up with this life. At that time due to the drinking habit of his father and his ways – he divorced his wife and Rahul put his head on my shoulders. Though, this was not just the only reason for him to come to me. He wanted to change his life. He said that I don't want to sit, think, grow old and die one day or be like his father. He would like to join the academy and do whatsoever that requires him to make big in life. I didn't forget those intense eyes even today and so I agreed to let him join the academy.

Those eyes didn't cry that day and didn't blink either. Such was the desire in him to change his circumstance that he told me that he will like to move from his village in Satara to Mumbai to get richer and famous and then from Mumbai to become an international body-builder. For once, I thought he must be kidding, and then after he had finished and I realized what he had said, he had already put his feet on to leave and with his back turned on me had left. He met me once again and this time was at the national championship a year later. He had won Gold for Mumbai that day and I was sure by then that he will achieve something big one day. How big I didn't know?

After four years of intense bodybuilding, I met him again and asked one day at the gym in Delhi where Commonwealth games 2010 were about to begin soon and where I was on the routine lookout for the best talents for that international event coming up. I asked- "Why aren't you resting like others". He replied Sir, "I want to represent India in the 2010 Commonwealth games and win nothing lesser than Gold. I will rest when all those people including my father who cast off me as good for nothing, hear me loud at the International arena and see me with a Gold medal."

Finally, I was surprised when I saw this boy achieve so much in life and still loving and testing life as if it's his first and last chance to change his condition- today or never. He has risen that high that now to spot him was much easier on a

Television than just meeting him. He was in all places and still so difficult to meet him personally. He is the one who didn't agree to a lesser life, worked each day to see that change in him, and still is not content to rest upon his achievements as if stopping and not improving further is a life not normal. It is a change to be bigger and better each day. It is to make a goal to become unbeaten and then make another goal to remain successful, and another to convert everyone who said a no to a yes because you never heard any no on you. It is now for you to leave nothing for a chance to be successful till it is in your habit to win each time.

He is today an actor, a wrestler, and a politician. He is successful and the best in all. I won't ask you who is he. Whether he is Sushil Kumar from India or Arnold Schwarzenegger of the USA is not important. To find you in their place is most important.

Moral of the story

Essential is what is the purpose that needs you to change so that you are counted among winners who stand up each time they fall and as each time you fall, you make a habit to rise again and finally make victory your only selection and not a chance.

Steps for making success a Habit and not a Chance

1. A repeated positive action or a visualization of a better present makes you feel better and each day you rehearsal on it becomes your habit. This in the long run when engaged further with utmost sincerity and belief in yourself leaves you with no chance to fail. This is how you become unbeaten. It all starts with self-realization towards this change. Change is first and rest is a chain reaction.

2. Chance is for the weak and to leave it to chance is like accepting your destiny that you are not eager to change. Changing your destiny is when you challenge it to change it as if destiny was also destined to change until you stopped. Think over it.

3. Success is itself deficient unless we change. It is the enthusiasm to rise to a higher life and self. Failures do not matter much till success has become a habit and failure becomes then just a matter of chance. There is nothing called a failure as it's another way of not doing something. Count the number of times you failed as the number of ways you learned of not doing something. This attitude of self-help to change yourself and

your situation is a success that should never breathe your last. It should outlive your age. Otherwise, we all know that failures are never final till we learn and success has an even shorter shelf life.

4. Unlearn your mistakes and do not repeat them. Take all precautions to be vigilant as you have all the rights in your pursuit of success. Leave no stone unturned to experiment and take the risk. Risk is another way of accepting a change that a lot of others have refused to take or it may be thought of as a change you are willing to take and move ahead where others have stopped.

5. Nothing will change unless you change. Your journey toward success is not only in its destination but in its run too. Don't leave it as an opening for many others just because you refused to open the door when it knocked the door to enter into your world. Your opportunity is your willingness to change not the world outside but your world inside.

Chapter 5

Your Story of action starts with a Change: My search within

This is my short story, the real one. It is unique in its many ways and the only character in this story is me. I am the champion of this story as other characters are my readers. Each of you has a story in you that you have to search within to bring a proper of you. Your story of action starts therefore when you change yourself and when you do so you see the world like never before just like the way I can see my world now. It's never too late to change but change is important, very important and my story has enough reasons for my readers to search for their own and will be when they search within.

I did my schooling from a reputed English medium and one of the few best schools in India. Thanks to my parents. Today, I realize how important it is for me to be able to write the way I am doing today. Those years at school were of virtuousness as maturity never took on until I entered college. The search for a change was a question for me from even those days at college as I was not pleased with one task and challenged myself into different activities – courses a better word in those days as they were many options to choose from or maybe even more today. Nevertheless, those courses didn't turn up much into what I wanted to do as by that time I had another and a better one- an MBA to land me into a desirable job.

Finally landing a job in customer services may not be the best of jobs from the public's viewpoint but I was now getting better with age. The search for a change continued further because my impatient mind was always searching for something I desired but wasn't very clear. This search was vague in my mind yet continued even years after being into the job of customer services, and rising to the level of a manager was however this time in a financial sector. In the pursuit to find meaning from life- where I was heading and why was becoming very important and I was clear in my mid-thirties that I was born to lead, to educate, and to create value for others. In the whole process, I never stopped learning new things to make sense out of my life.

This thought of value creation had surfaced and I could foresee much better now but in the worldly affairs of the family and running for it like many others- the journey continued including a lesser fulfilment with jobs even while I was at the top of my career at that time and respected by all alike. I was able to meet the expectations of many and all, while none of them could meet my own. It was not their fault because it was inside. A search unless taken within remains so vital. The job in hand was never an issue and I was bright enough to deliver my best, sometimes up to the mark and many times beyond however most of the time I had no time to think elsewhere. This elsewhere was nowhere but inside. I always choose on my own to quit the job unless I left for them a reason good enough for them to take such a decision. I was fortunate even to find another and this risk-taking ability in me was unlike in many others. I attribute this to my thirst to improve myself and to give a direction to my life into doing what I like, and not just liking it but delivering it to the world. I was aware of it by my early forties- though late; better late than never.

I don't have any regrets or think even the slightest of it and always pat myself on the right decisions I took. I do take ownership of my actions and till now I am satisfied with my decisions and take pride in them. None of my learning was a mistake nor was my decision. This acceptance is very important. This allowed me to change into what I wanted from life and what I am doing presently.

Today, I am writing as a certified creative writer. I am happy to be able to deliver my love of change to all you lovely people. I also run my channel on youtube WELCOME TO SCORE MORE that is into Motivation, Management, and Education for classes 6th to 8th in Maths and Science. My work is being liked by many viewers in just a short span of a few months since 2020 last year when I started, and I feel elated and blessed at the thought of it for which I thank all my viewers for it. I am today an open book for many to read and through this book want you all to open your book of change that's within you; you know it best and I would be the first and not the last one to read your story of change. You all have it in you. I am a You-Tuber and used YouTube to voice my opinions and educate the masses. I feel privileged to be able to manage all on my own including my blog in Blogger- Score more with Manu.

This search was long but the best I could do for myself. I wanted to change the life of many others and how, was through a self-search. This search never shaped well in the corporate world because I was unable to think beyond my hours of duty including commuting that was long and tiring to leave me with a lesser scope to think beyond my family and finally almost negligible for myself.

Thinking outside the box and doing something that brings value to others is so fulfilling no job can deliver unless you are into noble occupations of social services or a teacher or a doctor. In that sense your liking your job and doing it well may give you immense pleasure is just fine but it is for you to go deeper if there is something better of you for the world. Further, the risk of losing jobs is always in the minds of people. Covid – the pandemic of 2020 is a strong reason but that is not enough a reason for you not to take risks for the sake of doing something you always wanted. People say it is one's passion but I don't think that's completely true. It is to like what you do and that becomes your passion with time but it should be to do what you like and that will always remain with you and in you. It will leave you always ardent about it. You have to find yours.

If you are rich, will you wish to get more money? Yes, why not but you may not wish it all the time because it may not be your wish come true. My friends who are working with sincerity may be a compulsion because the corporate world operates in a mechanical way leaving less room for employees to reinvent themselves or search for what they are good at. Many know what they are good at however are unable to discover their true potential outside the mundane 9 to 5 job. The time or shift is not the trouble but if you are a victim of routine who wants to change. One can't escape change. It's there in you wanting to vent out. My story has ended now but started and will never end as it's outside the 9 to 5- time zone, any time zone as it's a zone I made for myself outside my comfort zone and a life I choose the way I wanted to anchor it. I am living in it each day. This has become my comfort.

Landing is not important, safety may be a concern but still lesser important as nothing is secure in this world. However, take-off is the most important. All the rest will follow and with time fall in place. My search within is my victory. This is my story. I want you to follow your victory in your job, maybe if it's outside your job or wherever. Anchor your life before it's too late for you to search. Your story is already being read by many others and you are utilized well and if paid accordingly in your job is for you to decide. I am sure you are made for things much beyond this. Change your story if you want to create something valuable to this world you longed for and could not. Time is running.

You don't need to change things outside or catch a train to find your story. Your story is your search within that you pen it down the way you want yourself to be read and not the way the world reads you. Till then keep searching, enjoy life, and don't settle for anything if it doesn't change or changes you. Search for the action you want to create and that action is within you.

Moral of the story

Unless you find your story to uplift yourself for a better world and not just for yourself is like a life half-lived. The search for a better you in an improved world should never stop. Even if you fail to find a better world, you will find a better of yourself in any world.

Steps to search for your Story of action that starts with a Change

1. You all are unique. Learn to contribute to your best potential. If your contribution is not worth in your firm or if your contribution is not the best you wanted to put, then change your present circumstances and if you cannot; think within yourself to move ahead.

2. Change is when you search where you stand presently and where you want to go.

3. Change yourself and start acting for your own story you wanted to tell the world. Let you see the world by your eyes and not you being seen from the world's eyes.

4. The quest to find your better inner-self may be in a lifetime. Don't regret it as an attempt for it is not vain. However, every attempt to stay outside it is a life wasted.

5. Your hunt for what you came to this life is your purpose of life. You should leave no stone unturned to achieve it. Success in it is not in your hands but trying to achieve it and be in it is a life utilized to its best and a life worth living for.

Chapter 6

Measuring success without Change is a repeated mistake

There was once a highly successful businessman. Success has a different meaning for different people we all know. His name was Vikram Joseph. He took all measures to run his business well and was dedicated like any true businessman in its interests. He did all to keep his clients and customers happy and his sales and turnover never ditched him.

He took great pride in himself. Even his competitors were unable to inhibit his success by any means. I worked as an employee in another firm as a service provider to him a few years ago in 2018. I am sure it was the month of June and I was handling a shipment that was a priority for him and had to reach California at any cost in the next 2 days. The shipment didn't board yet and the flight was about to leave in another 8 hrs. I told him we are sorry and it would be boarded the next day. You know all problems have a solution towards the end in customer services in the way of saying sorry for the inconvenience meted to you. He was furious to such an extent that he started abusing the company like any customer in his situation would have done. He was not ready to listen to the other side of the story but just have his shipment boarded the same day. He was ready to pay another 20% to start with and reached a maximum of 30%. He asked for my Regional head as he was not ready to talk to a mere manager at least by the tone of his voice. He was not settling for anything lesser than having his shipment dispatched.

I transferred his call and Vikram was so unthankful of it and could not wait anymore. When the call went to the Regional Head, the scuffle went further and took an awkward turn, and became an ego concern. I don’t know what happened that day on the call but this shipment didn’t go for sure and he refused to do any further business with us. We still had many clients to serve and we did serve many more and continue doing so. At some point in life, one has to say no with a reason for doing so.

The year during the pandemic times in 2020, I met one of his ex-employees who were earlier reluctant to tell about the fate of the firm but then I somehow used my skills to ask him about Vikram and he was no more hesitant for an exchange over lunch if the bill was on my plate and I agreed upon it. This person was snubbed in full public glare and was even told by his guards that he be pushed out physically if necessary as he explained his plight. He said this temper in Vikram was not new, just that this time I was his victim. He further explained that the firm is not operational anymore because he had run into legal issues with a lot of employees including service providers just like us. He said there was something unusual in him like a split personality. He was so well-behaved with his clients and always scored so well with them while he was so nasty with his employees and his service providers that it seems it backfired on him. Today, he does not even have enough money to start any new venture or pay any dues to any of the service providers or employees he hated most. How you sow, so shall you reap seems to be so true in his story.

Moral of the story

Your behaviour, attitude is your destiny that can make you or destroy you. Change has to be a change for all. You cannot be good to one at the loss of another. You can't expect to be a winner by favouring one section of people and disrespecting another section of your employees- the internal ones who love your firm may not love with the same force as your love for it and a little lesser may be. Your run will never be a longer one unless you make other's life as comfortable and respectful as you want your life to be with them. Your measure of success is not in the success of yours alone but in how many lives you touched.

Steps to know how much you achieved.

1. How successful you are is by how much you monitor, evaluate and control your success. It's not just the money you grow but the lives of many others to whom you interact and inspire. The change is not just in data all can see and read but also in the love and the respect you draw in the hearts of many and how you maintained and then sustained as a a reflection of your relations with them will never go unnoticed.

2. Success is by being happy and making others feel happy to work with you.

3. The Measure is a benchmark of your success that directs the change you desire to see in yourself and others. Others may be your firm, its employees, service providers, clients, and the general view of your stakeholders for you. It has to be ingrained and again periodically. It has to remain rooted and integral just like your character that remains righteous under all odds. This builds your character further and develops trust and a liking for you. All this needs a tremendous temperament and change within. This is the true measure of your success. It's like a true love that never goes wrong. Change- Measuring how much you achieved will never then fade.
4. The measure ensures you achieve the desired outcomes. Any variance once detected is also a

measure and then the correction begins. You cannot correct anything unless you measure its success or the degree of its variation. Satisfaction for an actor is only absolute if his audience is entertained and viewers are happy and speak in praise about him. This measure is sometimes relative and independent of the revenues that the film crosses or even if it performs lesser than the expectations or at worst if runs in losses. You are still up for another take. This is very similar to the satisfaction and guarantees you offer to your clients and if you can convert the same level of liking for your employees is a measure of your success. Success is a measure of the change you bring in the lives of many others and how you made them feel of their contribution. It can start by being just thankful to them. This is always more than the material wealth you get your hands on because, with this skill you acquire, you will never stop to obtain big in whatever undertaking you take in life and in business too. Vikram counted on his clients and never on his employees. It's a high time we realize the importance of clients and employees alike as the mcasurc of your flight is how higher and smoother you fly and is when you give equal gear to your employees and your clients.

5. The services rendered are a by-product of your product delivered and if taken seriously can change the stance towards its users irrespective of

some technical glitches. It has changed their outlook many times. Firms like Honda and Toyota had their products recalled too even if a far lesser number of times than by other firms. It is the brand loyalty through excellence in customer satisfaction built over the years. Measure what you have in you for a measure of your success. Unless you create value for others and respect their abilities, value their honesty in you, technical glitches can always wait and have waited to be corrected without any major loss of customers or goodwill. All these changes when happens are like a mistake never repeated as if never any mistake happened. Such are the stories of the big giants, if they can do so can you.

Chapter 7

Change is permanent and forever

There was once a tribe in the forests of the Western Ghats, south of Mumbai. They worshipped Trees and thought it was their birthright to protect them. I represent one of the trees they worshipped and protected. They believed that the protection of flora would ensure the longevity of their tribal clan. Many traditions in India are belief systems passed from one generation to another. In their forests, some anti-social elements had entered. On learning that they were Elephants and Tigers in the forest, those anti-social elements as six of them were armed men who were determed to poach those animals for fun and commercial reasons. In one of their searches far and deep in the jungles was when they came face-to-face in front of the tribes.

Initially, they tried to escape by acting as if they had lost their way when one of their men was caught running in fcar and that drcw thc attcntion of the tribe towards those men. They could stink the foul play and evil intent of those men that made the tribal men annoyed and they caught and blindfolded the men to present them in front of their head. This was a moment of fear for those men, who were too less in number and were outnumbered by the tribesmen that stood at 100.

Those six men were searched from head to foot to confirm the motive of their presence in the deep jungles. Finally, after an extensive search, there was a gun that was taken out from the pocket of one. First, the tribe felt the gun by the touch of it and later smelled it like black leather if that was, and then passed the weapon from one hand to another. They could not make out what this weapon was all about and made funny faces in surprise. The innocence of their ignorance had no limits.

The six men felt the blood running again in their veins as a new life unleashed and were sure that the attention of the tribes was now more on that object than the intention behind their move. They were convinced that the fools would set them free or maybe if they get an opportunity to flee away; they would not be going to miss any chance of it. I was helpless to whisper anything great to the tribesmen however I was sure that their love for me would witness the change in me and unmask the evil motives of the men.

The tribes danced and continued making some funniest faces on earth one could imagine that was of a much surprise and more than that a horror for them that they had kept to themselves. They were unfaltering to think that the tribe may be happy with them. They thought that instead of punishing us it looks as if they were in praise of us. They all together made a plan that while the tribe is merry and dancing to the wild tunes that are deafening their ears should end very soon as they would enter with the tribe dancing with them and slowly than would move in with them to elope later.

I was witnessing all this with a sad look for the times that had changed however this was not visible to those six men but surely was noticeable to the tribe as the tribesmen that day understood my plight when I was not moving much of my branches to their tunes. Who says trees don't feel as if it's just a privilege of the humans.

Now all of the six men entered the clan and started dancing. They felt light as they thought that they would now get plenty of time to escape. While those six men danced in merry, there was a silence. The men also stopped dancing. This was an intense moment of fear for the six men and they hated this instant and cursed it beyond imagination. It was for the first time in their lives when they felt that they are in trouble. They indeed were. Finally, they were handcuffed with ropes and beaten almost to death, and with blood all over on their body, they were left at the mercy of the doctors.

What exactly happened was funny but how was the tribe able to make out that the six men came to poach the animals without even speaking to them.

The fundamental law of nature is change and change is forever. It is this change that was noticed in the non-verbal cues of the animals and plants to which the tribes were so well attached and often spoke to them whenever they danced between them in merry. It was almost a custom they did daily and they would always hear birds chirping, animals making crazy sounds in return though better than theirs.

This was difficult for the urban man and especially poachers whose love for nature is selfish and who would never love an animal or plant with the same intensity as the tribes. The branches of the trees that day stopped to swirl, birds did not chirp in merry with the tribe, and neither any animal came out to investigate as usual. These guests were no guests but intruders for the tribe and they had enough reasons therefore to declare war with the six men and punish them. This change was never witnessed earlier and was against the law of nature as it was highly unlikely that the animals won't come out or the branches of trees won't swirl to and fro as they did each time.

Their love for nature was pure and was never abandoned. It was like a true love that can never go wrong. Ultimately, the six men got a beating of their lifetime and realized that change is not something which is seen by eyes only but that which may be felt too. The tribe's love for nature was seen in the way they connected with the animals and plants and that remained permanent and forever. The change in the city is not of connection and bonding. It is not selfless to protect but to make use of it for their very best. Even the plants and animals that are cut down and animals slaughtered in the name of development, food, and leather. The urban change is like a love gone wrong while the tribal men's love for nature has tested all the odds of time that has remained faithful in their love for plants and animals.

Moral of the story

The change lasts longer and forever if it is selfless and in the protection of others. Even mother, nature comes to the rescue wherever she sees selfless love for one another. It resonates. Change that creates a value for others blossoms in every heart and therefore never loses its shine. Your true colours are not in your show business but your meaningful business to the world.

Steps to attain change for an experience that is permanent and everlasting

1. It has to be from your heart and the benefit to others as pure and real just like if that was for your own. Change may not be visible to the eyes but the quintessence of it is to bring a lasting impact on the lives of many others even if far-fetched and not seen but can be felt. The six men could not see the love of the tribe for nature and vice-versa but it was there and forever just like your closed eyes that cannot see the sun and still feel its presence by its shine on you. On the other hand, it was not only seen but even felt by the tribe and nature alike. It is the objective to feel the change that matters and not always its results.

2. Love can also go wrong. It can either bind us together or separate us. A person who fails to cherish love around him and therefore without any due respect to love eventually dies without love and no responsibilities. Your responsibilities should be undertaken for your need to change so that you live and die for what you love the most.

3. Change is ageless and can never mislead you unless you don't wish to change.

Change is never a skill issue but often a will issue. Make yourself strong to create a skill in you that can change you and the people around you.

4. Never quit or lose hope. Have faith that tomorrow would always be a better day and work tirelessly to improve your present for a better future for yourself and many others.

5. Brainstorm and keep working on ways to change keeping development in mind. You will always then embrace change as a love that never will leave you, just as the love of the tribal men towards nature that remained forever and permanent like the change itself.

Conclusion

Your success is in the achievement of many others. The moment you change your life is the time your moment has come and is when you will come to action that will take you far away from daydreaming. Dreams become a reality with such an action that is selfless and then you get even more than what you asked for. Change is always permanent and pervasive in all beings. The day you change yourself is when you realize your purpose in life and any action you do to achieve that purpose is incomplete if without a change. Change, therefore, is real and like true love. It is not a matter of chance but a chosen habit that empowers you each day. It corrects and empowers you to produce another product out of you that is a newer you from within as a measure of how much you achieved. What is a success then? Frankly speaking, it is your search for yourself and your love of life that likes change so that you live a life that is so impactful and you in it so resourceful. That you are remembered for the changes you brought in your lifetime and the lives you touched is your measure of success. It is my success too.

Positive Affirmations of Change from the book

- *Change is from within.*
- *Change is always permanent and pervasive in all beings.*
- *Changes you brought in your lifetime and the lives you touched are your measure of success.*
- *The moment you change your life is the time your moment has come.*
- *The change in the city is not of connection and bonding.*
- *Change never comes easy and has a price of discomfort to pay.*
- *Change outside, inside, and everywhere that has always existed and will remain forever as the fundamental law of nature.*
- *In just knowing what they are missing is good enough for them to change.*
- *Resist Change to invite miseries.*

- ***The Measure is a benchmark of your success that directs the change you desire to see in yourself and others.***

- ***Changing your destiny is when you challenge it to change it as if destiny was also destined to change until you stopped.***

- ***It measures you in your lifetime; your willingness to change and your change for a better you is a stronger you in a living you, who didn't just compromise to exist.***

- ***Change is a much happier you.***

- ***Change is a destiny re-lived wherein you are the audience as well as the actor.***

- ***It may make you a winner or a loser but you will be always remembered for the hope that you ignited in the lives of many others.***

Epilogue

I, **Manu Gandhi**, also the protagonist, in my book **Change- Measuring how much you achieved** attempts to bring out the best in you. It attempts to explain each chapter through stories that revolve around the subject of Change. Why it is so important for you and me? Our apprehensions toward change are normal as our routine is life so comfortable we don't want to mess with it. Still, we lead a life that changes each passing day and the stories are well woven into the fabric of change leaving you with reasons to do so. Each chapter is a story with morals and further steps on how you can achieve change that you can cherish, embrace and live a life of change that is so fulfilling and full. I, as a protagonist, am also a narrator who is well connected to the key character in each of the stories is the highlight of the narrative. Further, and somewhere readers will find my story inside too.

www.ingramcontent.com/pod-product-compliance
Ingram Content Group UK Ltd.
Pitfield, Milton Keynes, MK11 3LW, UK
UKHW041643190726
13854UKWH00006B/2664

9 798717 149396